•BAKE *and* MAKE•
AMAZING
CAKES

Written by Elizabeth MacLeod
Illustrated by June Bradford

KIDS CAN PRESS

With lots of love to all my wonderful aunts:
Aunt Alix, Aunt Betty, Aunt Dorothy, Aunt Dot,
Aunt Louise, Aunt Marj, Aunt Mary Lou, Aunt Riek,
Aunt Tod, and in memory of Aunt Helen – E.M.

Text © 2001 Elizabeth MacLeod
Illustrations © 2001 June Bradford

KIDS CAN DO IT and the logo are trademarks of Kids Can Press Ltd.

Kids Can Press acknowledges the financial support of the Government of Canada,
through the BPIDP, for our publishing activity.

Published in Canada by   Published in the U.S. by
Kids Can Press Ltd.   Kids Can Press Ltd.
29 Birch Avenue   2250 Military Rd.
Toronto, ON M4V 1E2   Tonawanda, N.Y. 14150

Edited by Lori Burwash
Designed by Karen Powers
Photography by Frank Baldassarra
Cakes by June Bradford
Printed in Hong Kong by Wing King Tong Company Limited

The hardcover edition of this book is smyth sewn casebound.
The paperback edition of this book is limp sewn with a drawn-on cover.

CM 01 0 9 8 7 6 5 4 3 2 1
CM PA 01 0 9 8 7 6 5 4 3 2 1

Canadian Cataloguing in Publication Data

MacLeod, Elizabeth
Bake and make amazing cakes

(Kids can do it)
ISBN 1-55074-849-1 (bound)   ISBN 1-55074-848-3 (pbk.)

1. Cake — Juvenile literature. I. Bradford, June. II. Title. III. Series.

TX771.M333 2001   j641.8653   C00-931788-0

Kids Can Press is a Nelvana company

Contents

Introduction

*Stars, castles, tigers and dinosaurs —
it's easy to create cakes in all these shapes
and many more. Cakes make any
celebration special. Even an everyday
dinner becomes an occasion when you
finish it with a cake you've made and
decorated yourself. Cakes are wonderful
presents for friends and family, too.*

*Once you've made the cakes in this book,
try creating other cakes in whatever
shapes you like. You'll be surprised at how
easy it is to bake great-looking cakes —
you might say it's a piece of cake!*

CAKE RECIPES

Most projects in this book use one or
two cakes; a few use cupcakes. To make
the cakes and cupcakes, follow the easy
recipes on pages 32 to 36. Or use a
cake mix and follow the directions on
the package.

MIXING CAKES

For most cakes, you must beat the
batter with a hand or electric mixer to
make a light cake with a good texture.
If you don't have a mixer, beat the
batter by hand until it is smooth.

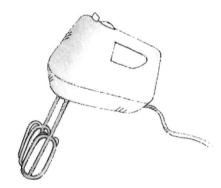

CAKE PANS

Cakes can be baked in almost any
container that safely goes in the oven.
It's a good idea to line the containers
with aluminum foil, shiny side up. The
foil makes the cakes easy to remove
from the pans, and the shiny surface
helps prevent the cakes from burning.

Line cupcake pans with cupcake papers. (Be sure to remove the papers before you cut and decorate the cupcakes.)

BAKING CAKES

Bake cakes in the center of your oven, no more than two at a time. To check if a cake is done, insert a toothpick or cake tester into the middle. If the toothpick comes out clean and dry, the cake is ready. Or gently touch the middle. If it springs back and the sides have shrunk away from the pan, the cake is done.

BAKING TIMES

Cooking times vary from oven to oven. Bake your cakes for the minimum time suggested, then test to see if they're done. If they're not, check them again in a few minutes. You may want to set a timer to remind you.

COOLING CAKES

Wearing oven mitts, remove the cake from the oven and place it on a cooling rack for at least 5 minutes. Then turn the cake upside down onto the cooling rack and remove it from the pan and foil. Let the cake cool completely before you cut and ice it.

Use a thick pair of oven mitts to handle hot cake pans. Always ask an adult to help you when moving cake pans into and out of the oven.

ICING CAKES

To make icing, follow the easy recipes on pages 37 and 38. Or buy ready-made icing or an icing mix and follow the directions on the package.

Before you begin icing, it's a good idea to cut the cake and let it stand for 1 to 2 hours. This allows the cut edges to dry out a little and makes the cake easier to ice.

To ice your cake, start by placing a dollop of icing on it. With a table knife, use short strokes to spread the icing from the top of the dollop — this keeps crumbs from getting in the icing. Continue adding dollops and icing this way until the cake is thickly covered. If your icing is hard to spread, dip the knife in hot water.

You can use icing to make the corners of your cake squarer, the edges straighter or the top rounder. (You can also use a knife to even out your cake before you begin icing.)

DECORATING CAKES

You can find candy, sprinkles, colored sugar and tinted icing at grocery stores, bulk-food stores or cake-decorating stores. Choose candies with strong colors. Light-colored candies look best on dark icing and dark candies look good on light-colored icing. See pages 39 and 40 for other decorating ideas and page 37 for how to tint icing.

MELTING CHOCOLATE

Use melted chocolate chips or bars of semisweet or milk chocolate to decorate your cake. If you break the bars into small pieces, the chocolate will melt faster.

Chocolate burns easily, so ask an adult to help you carefully melt it in a microwave or double boiler. Heat the chocolate just enough to melt it, then let it cool slightly before you use it. If the chocolate begins to harden before you are finished, melt it again.

DRAWING AND WRITING ON CAKES

It's easy to write a message or draw lines on your cake. Pour icing or slightly cooled melted chocolate into a small, heavy plastic bag, such as a freezer bag. When the bag is partly filled, snip off a tiny piece of one bottom corner.

Twist the bag closed and hold it firmly shut. Squeeze it until some chocolate or icing comes out. Cut a bigger hole if you want more to flow out.

DISPLAYING CAKES

Read each project and estimate how large your finished cake will be. If you can't find a plate or tray big enough to display your cake, use a large piece of heavy cardboard covered with aluminum foil.

FREEZING CAKES

Some projects call for only one round cake. You can save the other cake by freezing it. When the cake is completely cool, carefully wrap it in aluminum foil or plastic wrap and place it in a rigid container. Wrap and pack cupcakes the same way.

Sweet heart

Here's a special dessert for Valentine's Day, Mother's Day or Father's Day.

YOU WILL NEED

- 1 cake baked in a 20 cm (8 in.) round pan
- 1 cake baked in a 23 cm (9 in.) square pan
- 2 recipes of white icing, tinted pink
- decorations
- a large serrated knife (use only with an adult's help), a table knife

1 If the cakes aren't the same height, use the large knife to even them.

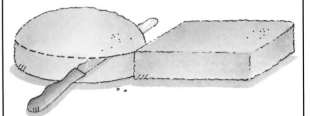

2 With the large knife, cut the round cake in half, as shown.

3 With the table knife, spread icing on both cut edges. Place one half so its cut side lies along one side of the square cake. Put the other half along an adjacent side of the square cake. If the cut edges of the halves are longer than the sides of the square cake, trim them.

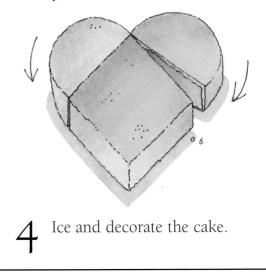

4 Ice and decorate the cake.

Terrific tiger

What a grrreat cake!
Try making any face you like.

YOU WILL NEED

- 1 cake baked in a
  20 cm (8 in.) round pan

- 1 recipe of white icing, tinted orange

- decorations, including 2 round cookies,
  2 large green gumdrops, black shoestring
  licorice, gumdrops, marshmallows,
  uncooked spaghetti,
  melted chocolate (page 7)

- a large serrated knife (use only with an
  adult's help), a table knife, a plastic bag

1 With the large knife, cut the cake diagonally, as shown.

2 Stack the pieces so the thick edges are on top of each other.

3 Use the table knife to ice the cake.

4 Place the round cookies at the top of the cake for ears.

5 To make the eyes, see page 39.

6 Use gumdrops or other candies to make the nose and mouth. Put two marshmallows below the nose, and carefully stick pieces of spaghetti into them for whiskers.

7 Draw on stripes with the melted chocolate.

Lucky rainbow

*Wish a friend happy birthday
with this colorful rainbow.*

YOU WILL NEED

- 1 cake baked in a
20 cm (8 in.) round pan
- 1 recipe of white icing
- decorations, including lots of
different-colored candies, such as
jelly beans or gumdrops
- a large serrated knife (use only with
an adult's help), a table knife

1   With the large knife, cut
the cake in half.

2   With the table knife, ice the top
of one half and place the other
half on top.

3   Stand the cake with the cut side
down and ice all sides.

4   Using the candies, cover the cake
in bands of each color.

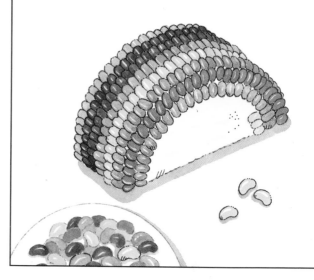

OTHER IDEAS

• Make a puppy by following steps 1 to 3, using icing tinted yellow.

Add floppy paper ears, gumdrop eyes and nose and a shoestring licorice mouth and tail. If you like, cover the puppy in tinted coconut (page 39).

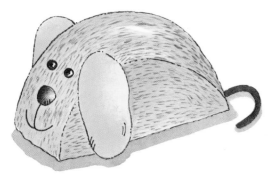

• You can make a cat, rabbit or mouse the same way.

• To make a watermelon, follow steps 1 and 2. Leave a small amount of the remaining icing white, tint a slightly larger amount green and color most of it pink. Ice the curved edge green, then stand the cake on that edge.

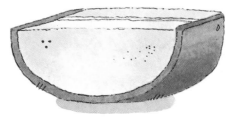

Ice a thin band white just inside the green icing.

Ice the rest of the cake pink and add chocolate chips for watermelon seeds.

Bright butterfly

Make this fun, easy cake to celebrate a perfect summer day.

YOU WILL NEED

- 1 cake baked in a 20 cm (8 in.) round pan
- 1 recipe of white icing, tinted any colors you like
- decorations, including black shoestring licorice
- a kitchen knife, a table knife

1 With the kitchen knife, cut a pointed oval from the cake.

2 Place the larger pieces, cut sides out, on either side of the oval body.

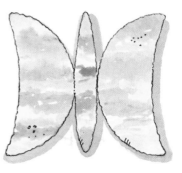

3 With the table knife, ice the body. Ice the wings a different color.

4 Decorate the cake, using the licorice as antennae.

OTHER IDEAS

- Make marble cakes by dividing half the batter for a white cake evenly into two prepared pans. Tint the remaining batter whatever color you like (page 33), then drizzle it in equal amounts into the two pans. With a table knife, lightly swirl the colored batter through the white.

Frothy mugcakes

When it's cold outside, serve these cupcakes with big mugs of cocoa.

YOU WILL NEED

- butter
- 1 recipe of cake batter
- 1 recipe of white icing
- ground cinnamon, miniature marshmallows
- 10 heavy ovenproof mugs, 2 shallow baking pans, a cooling rack, a table knife

1 Preheat the oven to 180°C (350°F).

2 Coat the inside of each mug with a thin layer of butter. Half fill each mug with batter.

3 Place the mugs in the baking pans. Have an adult place the pans in the oven and bake for 15 to 20 minutes or until done. Follow the directions for baking cakes on page 5, then place the mugcakes on the cooling rack.

4 When the mugcakes are completely cool, use the table knife to add a dollop of icing on top of each one, so that it looks like whipped cream.

5 Sprinkle cinnamon on the icing and add miniature marshmallows.

Cuddly cat

You can make this cake look like your favorite cat.

YOU WILL NEED

- 2 cakes baked in 20 cm (8 in.) round pans
- 1 recipe of white icing, tinted any color you like
- decorations, including 2 large green or yellow gumdrops, black shoestring licorice, a gumdrop, 2 round cookies
- a kitchen knife, a table knife

1 With the kitchen knife, cut one cake as shown.

2 Arrange these pieces around the other cake as shown.

3 With the table knife, use the icing to "glue" the pieces together, then ice the cake.

4 To make the eyes, see page 39.

5 Make a gumdrop nose, and use the licorice for the mouth and whiskers and the cookies for paws.

Cozy house

Welcome a new friend to your neighborhood with this house.

YOU WILL NEED

- 1 cake baked in a
23 cm x 33 cm (9 in. x 13 in.) pan

- 1 recipe of white icing,
tinted any color you like

- decorations, including fruit leather;
square, flat cereal; licorice;
melted chocolate (page 7)

- a large serrated knife (use only with
an adult's help), a table knife

1 With the large knife, cut the cake as shown.

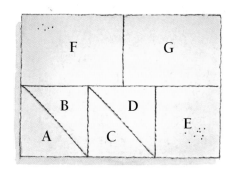

2 Assemble the pieces as shown. Use icing to glue the pieces together. Discard or eat the extra piece.

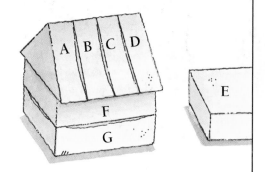

3 With the table knife, ice the whole house.

4 Decorate the house. If you like, add trees using upside-down ice-cream cones covered in green icing and green sugar or sprinkles.

OTHER IDEAS

- Use a half recipe of chocolate icing and a half of tinted white icing. Ice the roof with chocolate icing and the rest of the house with tinted icing.

Haunted castle

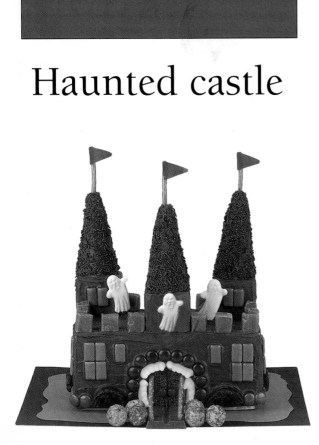

Don't be afraid to make this spooky cake.

YOU WILL NEED

- 1 cake baked in a
23 cm x 33 cm (9 in. x 13 in.) pan

- 2 recipes of chocolate icing

- decorations, including
fruit leather, 5 straight pretzels,
3 pointed ice-cream cones,
chocolate sprinkles,
caramels, a bar of chocolate
or cookies

- a large serrated knife
(use only with an adult's help),
a table knife, a kitchen knife

1 With the large knife, cut the cake as shown. Discard or eat one of the small pieces.

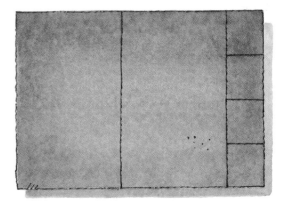

2 Assemble the cake as shown. With the table knife, use the icing to attach the small pieces.

3 Set aside a small amount of icing for steps 4 and 5. With the rest, ice the entire castle, keeping any straight edges as straight as possible.

4 With the kitchen knife, cut a flag out of fruit leather and use icing to attach it to a pretzel. Gently poke the pretzel through the tip of an ice-cream cone. Repeat with the other cones.

5 Stand the ice-cream cones upside down on your work surface and ice them. Cover them with sprinkles.

6 Place the cones on the towers.

7 Arrange the caramels along the top of the castle.

8 Decorate your castle. Make a drawbridge with a bar of chocolate or cookies. Use the remaining pretzels as drawbridge chains.

OTHER IDEAS

• Make a fantasy castle by icing the cake with white icing and decorating it with light-colored miniature marshmallows, sprinkles and other decorations.

Christmas tree

Here's the perfect dessert for a Christmas party.

YOU WILL NEED

- 1 cake baked in a 23 cm x 33 cm (9 in. x 13 in.) pan
- 1 recipe of white icing, tinted green
- decorations
- a large serrated knife (use only with an adult's help), a table knife

1 With the large knife, cut the cake into three triangles, as shown.

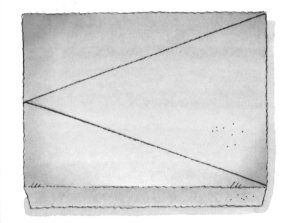

2 Form one large triangle with the two small triangles.

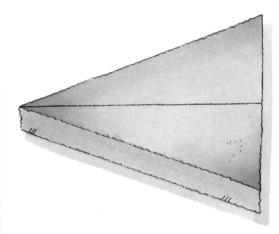

3 With the table knife, ice the top of this triangle.

4 Place the other triangle on top and ice the cake. If you like, sprinkle green sugar and sprinkles or coconut tinted green (page 39) over the cake.

5 Decorate the cake.

Spring flowers

*Bake a whole bouquet of
these pretty flowers.*

YOU WILL NEED

- 12 cupcakes
- 1 recipe of white icing
- food coloring
- decorations
- a kitchen knife, a table knife

1 With the kitchen knife, cut six evenly spaced notches around a cupcake. Repeat with seven other cupcakes. Discard or eat the notches you cut away.

2 Tint two-thirds of the icing whatever color you'd like your flowers to be. You can make each flower a different color if you like. With the table knife, ice and decorate the flowers.

3 Cut one of the remaining cupcakes in half horizontally. Cut each half into two leaf shapes. Repeat with the other three cupcakes.

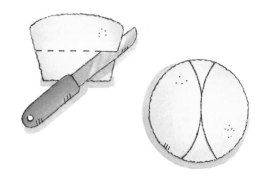

4 Tint the remaining icing green. Ice and decorate the leaves. Place two leaves with each flower.

Makes 8 flowers

Shining star

You'll be a star when you serve this terrific cake.

YOU WILL NEED

- 2 cakes baked in 20 cm (8 in.) round pans
- 1 recipe of white icing, tinted yellow
- decorations
- 10 toothpicks, a kitchen knife, a table knife

1 Evenly space five toothpicks around the edge of one cake. Place a circle of five toothpicks about 4 cm (1½ in.) inside the first circle, with each toothpick halfway between two outer toothpicks.

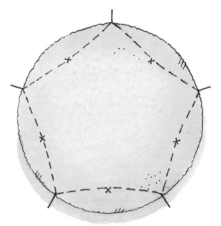

2 With the kitchen knife, cut from each outer toothpick to the two inner toothpicks closest to it. Remove the toothpicks and repeat steps 1 and 2 with the other cake. Discard or eat the pieces you cut away.

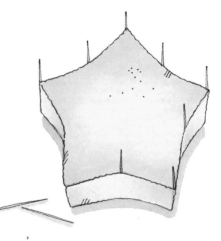

3 With the table knife, ice the top of one star and place the other star on top so that the points line up. Ice and decorate your cake.

Easter bunny

Celebrate Easter or spring with this bunny. Try making it with carrot cake and cream cheese icing, too.

YOU WILL NEED

- 2 cakes baked in 20 cm (8 in.) round pans
- 1 recipe of white icing
- food coloring
- decorations, including black shoestring licorice
- a kitchen knife, a table knife

1 With the kitchen knife, cut one cake as shown.

2 Arrange these pieces around the other cake as shown.

3 Tint a small amount of icing any color you like, and use the table knife to ice the bow tie.

4 Ice the rest of the cake with the white icing.

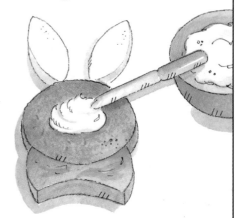

5 Use licorice and other candies to decorate your bunny. Decorate the bow tie, too.

Rolling bus

Beep! Beep!
Make way for this delicious cake!

YOU WILL·NEED

- 1 cake baked in a
23 cm x 33 cm (9 in. x 13 in.) pan
- 1 recipe of white icing, tinted yellow
- decorations, including 4 round cookies,
fruit leather, black shoestring licorice,
licorice sticks, 4 round candies
- a large serrated knife (use only with
an adult's help), a table knife

1 With the large knife, cut the cake
in half lengthwise, as shown.

2 Cut about 7.5 cm (3 in.) off an
end of one piece of cake.

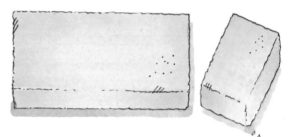

From this small piece,
cut a strip 2.5 cm
(1 in.) thick.

Cut this strip in half lengthwise. Save
one of these strips. Discard or eat the
other one.

3 With the table knife, ice the top of the largest piece of cake. Place the next largest piece on top, lining up the pieces at one end. Ice one long side of the strip of cake from step 2. Place it, icing side down, at the other end of the top piece. Ice the cake.

4 Place the cookies around the cake base to make wheels.

5 Add windows using fruit leather. Make shoestring licorice wipers, and put shoestring licorice above and below the side windows.

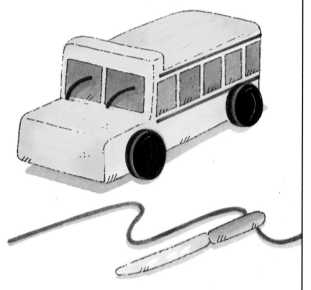

6 Use two short pieces of licorice stick for the front grill and one long piece for the bumper.

7 Place two round candies on either side of the grill for headlights. Put lights on the top strip, too.

Jack-o'-lantern

*What a great centerpiece for a
Halloween party. Or make a face,
planet Earth, a ball — anything round!*

YOU WILL NEED

- 1 recipe of cake batter
- 1 recipe of white icing, tinted orange
- decorations, including
  black shoestring licorice
- a 1.5 L (6 c.) round glass casserole dish
  lined with aluminum foil, a cooling rack,
  a large serrated knife (use only with an
  adult's help), a table knife

1 Preheat the oven to 150°C
(300°F).

2 Pour the cake batter into the
dish and bake for 60 to 70
minutes or until done. Follow the
directions for baking and cooling
cakes on page 5.

3 With the large knife, slice the
cake in half horizontally.

4 With the table knife, ice the top
of the flat layer. Place the
rounded layer on top and ice the
whole cake.

5 Make lines in the icing to look
like the lines on a pumpkin.
Add the eyes, nose and mouth using
shoestring licorice and other candies.

Teddy bear

This un-bear-ably cute cake can also be decorated to look like a panda or a snowman.

YOU WILL NEED

- 2 cakes baked in 20 cm (8 in.) round pans
- 1 recipe of chocolate icing
- decorations, including 6 flat, round chocolate cookies; 1 white or chocolate marshmallow; 2 small, round candies; a red gumdrop; black shoestring licorice
- a kitchen knife, a table knife

1 With the kitchen knife, cut a shallow groove from one cake. Discard or eat the piece you cut away.

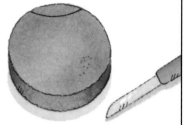

2 Arrange the cakes as shown.

3 With the table knife, ice the cake. If you like, sprinkle on chocolate sprinkles.

4 Place two cookies on the cake to make ears. Put smaller cookies on top if you like. Add cookie paws.

5 To make the eyes, see page 39.

6 Use the gumdrop for the nose and the licorice for the mouth and paws.

Delicious burger

A hamburger for dessert? Yum!

YOU WILL NEED

- 1 recipe of cake batter
- ½ recipe of white icing
- brown and yellow food coloring
- ½ recipe of chocolate icing
- 25 mL (2 tbsp.) strawberry jam
- round red gummi candies
- green fruit leather
- almonds, toasted (see "Note" on page 27)
- a 1.5 L (6 c.) round glass casserole dish lined with aluminum foil, a cooling rack, a large serrated knife (use only with an adult's help), a table knife, a kitchen knife, scissors

1 Preheat the oven to 150°C (300°F).

2 Pour the cake batter into the dish and bake for 60 to 70 minutes or until done. Follow the directions for baking and cooling cakes on page 5.

3 With the large knife, slice the cake horizontally into three equal layers.

4 Put aside a small amount of white icing. Tint the rest light brown. With the table knife, use about half the light brown icing to ice the sides of the bottom layer.

5 With the chocolate icing, ice the top of the bottom layer. Place the middle layer on top and ice its sides and top, also with chocolate icing.

6 Tint the white icing you set aside mustard yellow. Ice the edge of the middle layer to look like mustard.

7 Drizzle jam around the edge to add ketchup to your burger.

8 With the kitchen knife, cut gummi candies to look like tomato slices. Place around the edge of the middle layer.

9 For shredded lettuce, cut the fruit leather into thin strips with the scissors and place around the edge.

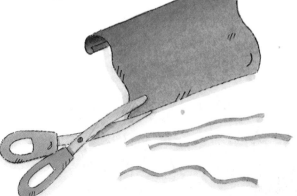

10 Place the rounded layer on top and ice it with the remaining light brown icing. Sprinkle on the almonds.

Note: *To toast almonds, preheat the oven to 150°C (300°F). Place the almonds on a cookie sheet and toast them for 3 minutes or until they are golden brown. Watch the almonds carefully — they burn easily.*

Creeping caterpillar

Did you ever think you'd eat a caterpillar?

YOU WILL NEED

- 12 cupcakes
- 1 recipe of white icing, tinted any colors you like
- decorations, including colored sugar or tinted coconut (page 39), black shoestring licorice, 2 lollipops
- a table knife

1 Arrange the cupcakes in a wavy line, tops down.

2 With the table knife, ice the cupcakes. You can make each cupcake a different color if you like. Cover them with colored sugar or tinted coconut.

3 Decorate your caterpillar. Use candies for a face, shoestring licorice for feet and lollipops for antennae.

OTHER IDEAS

- Use icing to stick the tops of two cupcakes together. Ice and decorate to look like an apple.

Sun hat

This hat is good enough to eat!
What other hats can you make?

YOU WILL NEED

- 2 cakes baked in 20 cm (8 in.) round pans
- 1 recipe of white icing, tinted any color you like
- decorations, including fruit leather or shoestring licorice, marshmallow flowers and leaves (page 39)
- a large serrated knife (use only with an adult's help), toothpicks, a kitchen knife, a table knife

1 With the large knife, slice one cake in half horizontally, as shown. Put one half aside for step 3. Discard or eat the other half.

2 Place a ring of toothpicks 2.5 cm (1 in.) in from the edge of the other cake. With the kitchen knife, cut along the ring. Remove the toothpicks. Discard or eat the cake you cut away.

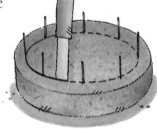

3 With the table knife, ice the top of the piece of cake from step 1. Place the other piece on top, in the center, and ice the whole cake.

4 Place a band of fruit leather or shoestring licorice around the hat. Add marshmallow flowers and leaves.

Scary dinosaur

Decorate this cake to look like your favorite dinosaur.

YOU WILL NEED

- 2 cakes baked in 20 cm (8 in.) round pans
- 1 recipe of white icing, tinted green
- decorations, including a licorice stick
- a kitchen knife, a short wooden skewer or long match with head removed, a table knife

1 With the kitchen knife, cut one cake as shown.

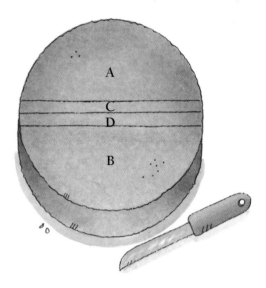

2 Cut off one-third of the other cake. From this piece, cut a curved strip about 2.5 cm (1 in.) wide. Cut a piece 7.5 cm (3 in.) long from this strip for the head and neck.

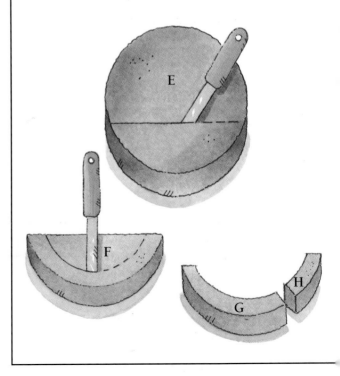

3 Cut a notch from the large piece of cake from step 2, as shown. Save the large piece and discard or eat the small piece.

E

5 With the table knife, ice the dinosaur, then decorate it. Use two short pieces of licorice for arms (you may have to fasten them to the cake with toothpicks).

4 Assemble the cake as shown, attaching the pieces with icing. To attach the head, insert the skewer into the cake at the notch and fit the neck onto the skewer. The tail is made from the strips you cut in step 1. Shape the head and tip of the tail, if you like.

Note: *Be sure to remove the skewer and any toothpicks before you serve the cake.*

G

E

B →

A

H

F

C
D

RECIPES

When you're baking cakes, it's very important to measure accurately and follow the instructions carefully.

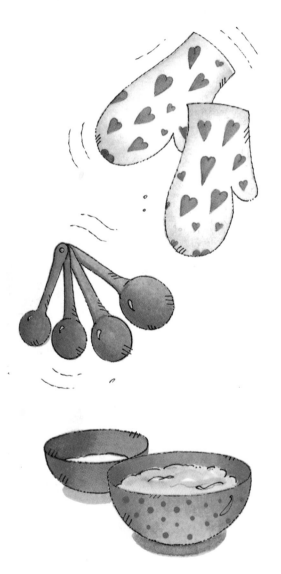

ABBREVIATIONS

The following abbreviations have been used in the recipes:

L = liter
mL = milliliter
cm = centimeter
°C = degrees Celsius
c. = cup
tbsp. = tablespoon
tsp. = teaspoon
in. = inch
°F = degrees Fahrenheit

MEASURING INGREDIENTS

Both the metric and imperial systems of measurement are used in this book. The systems vary, so choose one and use it for all your measuring.

Dry ingredients and wet ingredients require different measuring cups. A dry measuring cup is flat across the top so you can level off the dry ingredients with a knife for a really accurate measure.

A wet measuring cup has a spout to make pouring easier. Be sure to match your ingredients with the correct type of measuring cup.

White cake

450 mL	white sugar	1¾ c.
150 mL	butter or margarine, at room temperature	⅔ c.
2	eggs	2
10 mL	vanilla	2 tsp.
750 mL	all-purpose flour	3 c.
12 mL	baking powder	2½ tsp.
2 mL	salt	½ tsp.
375 mL	milk	1½ c.

measuring cups and spoons,
a large and a medium mixing bowl,
a hand or electric mixer, a sifter,
cake pan(s) lined with aluminum foil,
a cooling rack

1 Preheat the oven to 180°C (350°F).

2 In the large bowl, use the mixer to cream the sugar and butter until they are smooth and light in color. Add the eggs and vanilla. Blend well.

3 Sift together the flour, baking powder and salt into the medium bowl.

4 Add one-third of the dry ingredients to the wet mixture and mix well. Add half the milk and blend. Repeat, then add the remaining flour mixture and mix well.

5 Pour the batter into the pan(s) and push it out to the sides. Tap the pan(s) lightly to remove large air bubbles.

6 Place the pan(s) in the oven and bake for 30 to 40 minutes or until done (see "Baking Times" on page 5). Follow the directions for baking and cooling cakes on page 5.

Makes one 23 cm x 33 cm (9 in. x 13 in.) cake, two 20 cm (8 in.) round cakes, two 23 cm (9 in.) square cakes or 24 cupcakes

• To tint this batter, use food coloring. Start by adding three drops and keep adding drops until you create the color you want. Or stir about 50 mL (¼ c.) colored sugar into the batter.

• You can flavor this batter with extracts and flavorings, available at the grocery store. Start by adding three drops and keep adding drops until you create the flavor you want.

Chocolate cake

YOU WILL NEED

500 mL	white sugar	2 c.
150 mL	butter or margarine, at room temperature	2/3 c.
2	eggs	2
10 mL	vanilla	2 tsp.
625 mL	all-purpose flour	2½ c.
175 mL	cocoa powder	3/4 c.
12 mL	baking powder	2½ tsp.
2 mL	salt	½ tsp.
375 mL	milk	1½ c.

measuring cups and spoons,
a large and a medium mixing bowl,
a hand or electric mixer, a sifter,
cake pan(s) lined with aluminum foil,
a cooling rack

1 Preheat the oven to 180°C (350°F).

2 In the large bowl, use the mixer to cream the sugar and butter until they are smooth and light in color. Add the eggs and vanilla. Blend well.

3 Sift together the flour, cocoa, baking powder and salt into the medium bowl.

4 Add one-third of the dry ingredients to the wet mixture and mix well. Add half the milk and blend. Repeat, then add the remaining flour mixture and mix well.

5 Pour the batter into the pan(s) and push it out to the sides. Tap the pan(s) lightly to remove large air bubbles.

6 Place the pan(s) in the oven and bake for 30 to 40 minutes or until done (see "Baking Times" on page 5). Follow the directions for baking and cooling cakes on page 5.

Makes one 23 cm x 33 cm (9 in. x 13 in.) cake, two 20 cm (8 in.) round cakes, two 23 cm (9 in.) square cakes or 24 cupcakes

Banana cake

YOU WILL NEED

50 mL	milk	1/4 c.
15 mL	lemon juice	1 tbsp.
300 mL	white sugar	1 1/4 c.
125 mL	butter or margarine, at room temperature	1/2 c.
2	eggs	2
5 mL	vanilla	1 tsp.
500 mL	all-purpose flour	2 c.
5 mL	baking soda	1 tsp.
250 mL	mashed bananas (about 2 medium)	1 c.

measuring cups and spoons;
small, large and medium mixing bowls;
a wooden spoon; a sifter;
cake pan(s) lined with aluminum foil;
a cooling rack

1 Preheat the oven to 180ºC (350ºF).

2 In the small bowl, combine the milk and lemon juice. Set aside.

3 In the large bowl, use the wooden spoon to cream the sugar and butter until they are smooth and light in color. Add the eggs and vanilla. Beat until light and fluffy.

4 Add the milk mixture to the batter and beat well.

5 Sift together the flour and baking soda into the medium bowl.

6 Add one-third of the dry ingredients to the wet mixture and mix well. Add half the bananas and blend. Repeat, then add the remaining flour mixture and mix well.

7 Pour the batter into the pan(s) and push it out to the sides. Tap the pan(s) lightly to remove large air bubbles.

8 Place the pan(s) in the oven and bake for 40 to 50 minutes or until done (see "Baking Times" on page 5). Follow the directions for baking and cooling cakes on page 5.

Makes one 23 cm x 33 cm (9 in. x 13 in.) cake, two 20 cm (8 in.) round cakes, two 23 cm (9 in.) square cakes or 24 cupcakes

Carrot cake

Note: *If you want to use walnuts, first make sure no one is allergic to them.*

1 Preheat the oven to 180°C (350°F).

2 In the bowl, use the wooden spoon to cream the sugars and butter until they are smooth. Add the eggs, oil and vanilla. Blend well.

3 Sift together the flour, baking soda, cinnamon and salt into the wet mixture and mix.

4 Mix in the carrots, walnuts and raisins.

5 Pour the batter into the pan(s) and push it out to the sides. Tap the pan(s) lightly to remove large air bubbles.

6 Place the pan(s) in the oven and bake for 60 minutes or until done (see "Baking Times" on page 5). Follow the directions for baking and cooling cakes on page 5.

Makes one 23 cm x 33 cm (9 in. x 13 in.) cake, two 20 cm (8 in.) round cakes, two 23 cm (9 in.) square cakes or 24 cupcakes

White or chocolate icing

YOU WILL NEED

For white icing, you will need

1 L	icing sugar	4 c.

OR

For chocolate icing, you will need

750 mL	icing sugar	3 c.
250 mL	cocoa powder	1 c.

For both icings, you will also need

125 mL	butter or margarine, at room temperature	1/2 c.
75 mL	milk	1/3 c.
5 mL	vanilla	1 tsp.

measuring cups and spoons,
a sifter, a large mixing bowl,
a hand or electric mixer

1 Sift the icing sugar into the bowl. If you are making chocolate icing, sift the cocoa powder in as well. Add the butter and use the mixer to cream the butter and sugar together.

2 Add the milk and vanilla. Beat until smooth.

3 If the icing is too thin, add more icing sugar. If the icing is too thick, add a little more milk.

• If you want to tint white icing, use butter when making it — the coloring in margarine may affect the coloring you add. Use food coloring or icing color paste. If you use food coloring, start by adding three drops and keep adding drops until you create the color you want. If you use icing color paste, use a toothpick to add a very small amount of the paste. Add a little more until you create the color you want.

• You can flavor white and chocolate icing with extracts and flavorings, available at the grocery store. Start by adding three drops and keep adding drops until you create the flavor you want.

Icing will keep in a covered container in your refrigerator for about two weeks. Mix well before using and add a little milk or water if necessary.

Makes about 500 mL (2 c.)

Cream cheese icing

YOU WILL NEED

250 mL	cream cheese, at room temperature	1 c.
125 mL	butter or margarine, at room temperature	½ c.
1 L	icing sugar	4 c.
5 mL	vanilla	1 tsp.
5 mL	milk or orange juice	1 tsp.

measuring cups and spoons,
a hand or electric mixer,
a large mixing bowl, a sifter

1 Using the mixer, cream together the cream cheese and butter in the bowl.

2 With the mixer turned on, slowly sift the icing sugar into the bowl. Beat the mixture until there are no lumps.

3 Add the vanilla and milk. Beat until smooth.

4 If the icing is too thin, add more icing sugar. If the icing is too thick, add a little more milk.

If you like, add 15 mL (1 tbsp.) grated lemon or orange peel for extra flavor. Or add 125 mL (½ c.) chopped pecans.

This icing will keep in a covered container in your refrigerator for about one week. Mix well before using and add a little milk or water if necessary.

Makes about 500 mL (2 c.)

DECORATING IDEAS

MAKING EYES

• Make cat or tiger eyes by using a kitchen knife to slice the bottom off two green or yellow gumdrops. Place the slices on the face. Add a short piece of black shoestring licorice to each eye to make the center.

Or shape two round, black-centered licorice allsorts and place each on a candy fruit slice.

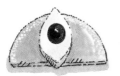

• To make teddy bear eyes, slice a marshmallow in half and place each half, cut side down, on a flat, round chocolate cookie. Place a small, round candy on each marshmallow.

TINTING COCONUT

• To tint coconut, place about 250 mL (1 c.) flaked coconut and 2 drops of food coloring in a jar. Tightly screw on the lid and shake the jar until the coconut is evenly tinted. Repeat with more food coloring if you want a darker color. To make brown coconut, use 15 mL (1 tbsp.) cocoa powder.

MAKING FLOWERS

• To make marshmallow flowers, use scissors to cut a marshmallow into five rounds, as shown. Use the pieces as petals to make flowers. Cut green marshmallows the same way for leaves.

USING CANDIES, NUTS AND OTHER DECORATIONS

- Birthday candles become really special when you place candy rings on top of your cake and insert each candle into a ring.

- For a fun birthday cake, use fruit leather to wrap a cake as if it's a present. Be sure to add a big bow!

- It's easy to decorate a cake by sprinkling nuts on the top or sides or both. (Before you do, make sure no one is allergic to nuts.) You can also crush peppermint candy or other hard candy and sprinkle it on your cake.

- Decorate a round cake to look like a drum. Add round lollipops for drumsticks.

- For a safari cake, ice the cake and place animal cookies around the outside and on top. Use coconut tinted green for grass.

CUTTING SHAPES

- Cut a cake into interesting shapes using large cookie cutters.

- Or cut the cake as shown. What other shapes can you cut?

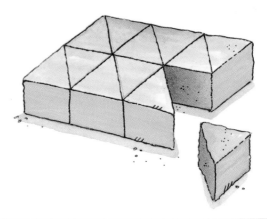

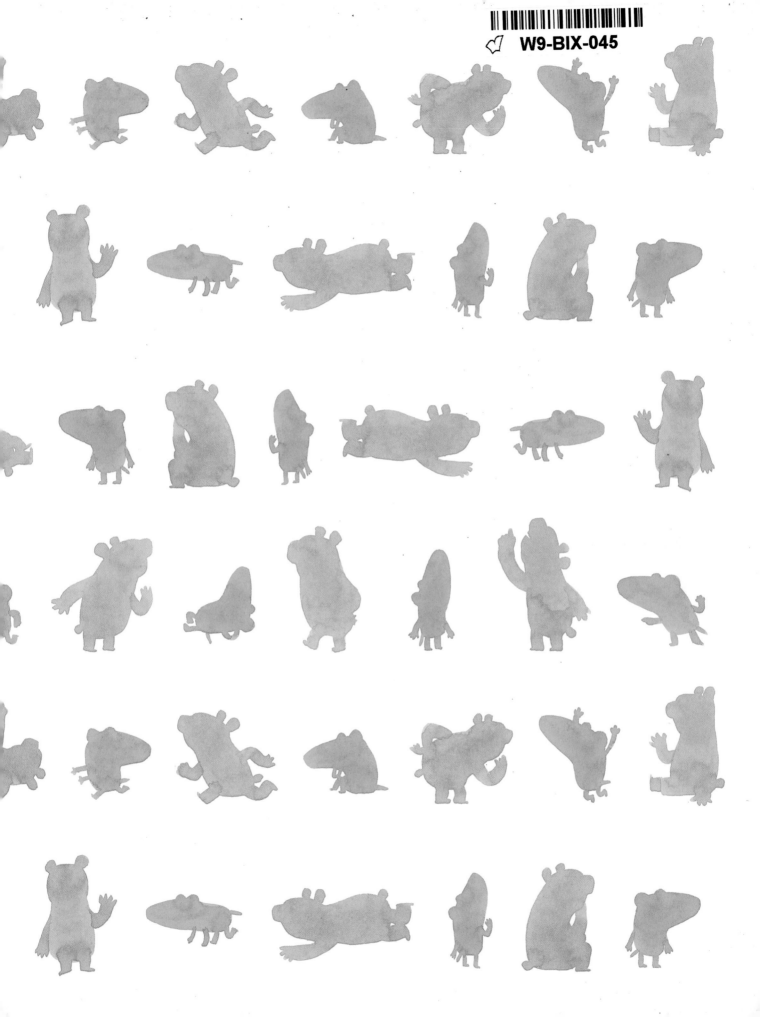

To Monika.
Daniel Fehr

A Big Help
Somos8 Series

© Text: Daniel Fehr, 2018
© Illustrations: Benjamin Leroy, 2018
© Edition: NubeOcho, 2018
www.nubeocho.com – hello@nubeocho.com

Text editing: Eva Burke and Rebecca Packard

Distributed in the United States by
Consortium Book Sales & Distribution

First edition: 2018
ISBN: 978-84-17123-21-5

Printed in China by Asia Pacific Offset,
respecting international labor standards.

A BIG HELP

Daniel Fehr
Benjamin Leroy

nubeOCHO

Badger sits alone on a stone.
Tears roll down his face.

"What's the matter?" asks Bear.

Badger does not answer. He only sobs.

After a long silence, Badger says, "I've lost my teddy."

"Hmm," says Bear. "Hmm," is all he says for quite a while.

But then Bear declares, "I can help!
I can find your teddy!"

Badger looks at Bear and tries to smile,
but he still looks sad.

First they search the meadow, because it's Badger's favorite place to play.

But Badger's teddy is not there; it's only Deer.

"Have you seen Badger's teddy?" asks Bear. "I'm helping to find it."

"No," says Deer. "I have not seen any teddies."

Then they search under the bushes, since things get lost easily in low and dark places.

But there is no teddy, only Hedgehog.

"Have you seen Badger's teddy?" asks Bear.
"I am helping to find it."

"No," says Hedgehog and rolls into a ball.

At the lake, they climb into a boat and paddle out to the middle of the water.

Maybe Badger lost his teddy while he was taking his morning bath.

Bear puts his head under the water.

But there is no teddy, only some fish.

Bear tries to ask his question, but he just makes bubbly sounds.

Not that it matters, since fish don't speak anyway.

Maybe Badger left his teddy at the big bush when he was picking some berries.

But there is no teddy, only some birds.

The birds are quite chatty and answer right away. But even they do not know where Badger's teddy is.

Near the forest, Bear and Badger climb a tree.

Maybe Badger's teddy got up there somehow.

When they reach the top, the tree
bends dangerously.

But there is no teddy, only Squirrel.

"Have you seen Badger's teddy?"
asks Bear. "I am helping to find it."

Squirrel squeaks and shouts:

"No! But please get off my tree!
You are too heavy for it!"

In the end, they return to the stone where Badger was sitting before.

Maybe they were looking too far away and Badger's teddy was here all along.

Bear lifts the stone.
But there is no teddy, only Worm.

"Have you seen Badger's teddy?" asks Bear.
"I am helping to find it."

"I don't see much down here, but I would
have noticed a teddy," says Worm.

Bear puts back the stone.
And sighs.
Twice.

"I am sorry," says Bear.
"I could not help you."

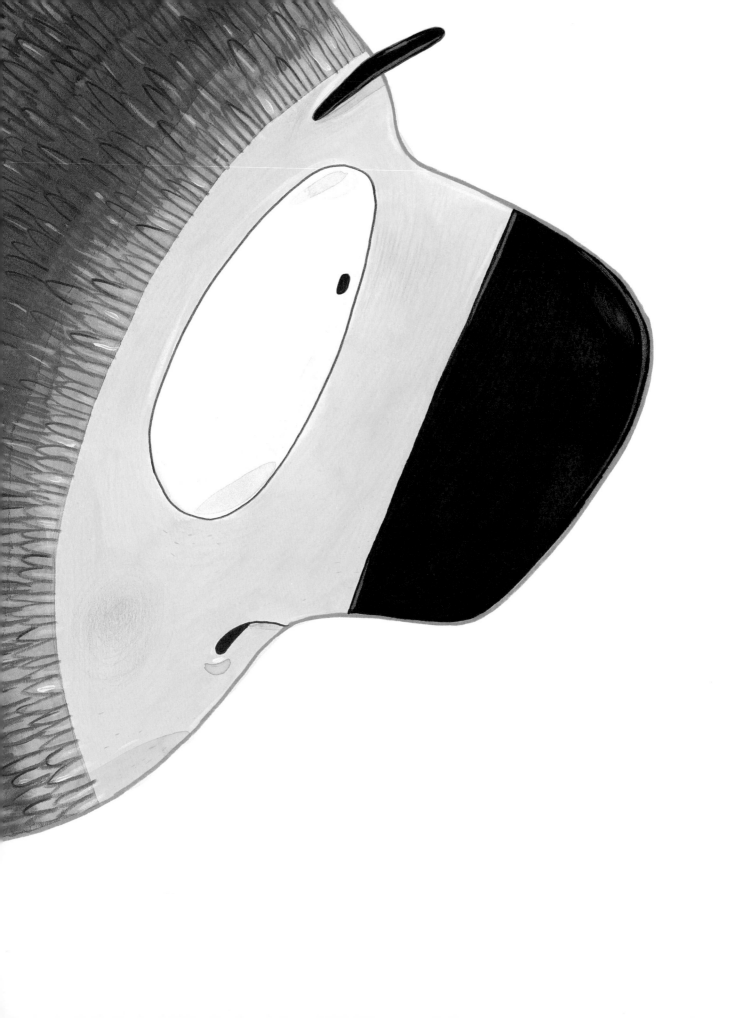

Badger looks at him
and asks,

"Help me with what?"

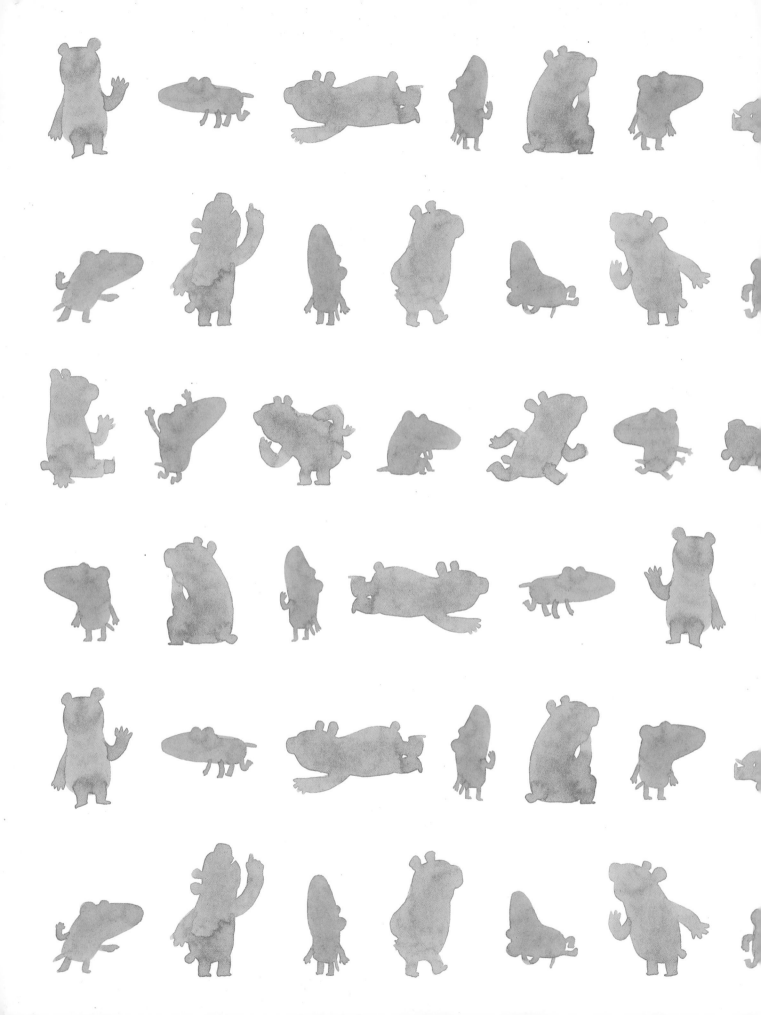